W9-BXV-991

Why Do Moving Objects Slow Down?
A Look at Friction

Jennifer Boothroyd

Lerner Publications

Minneapolis

Lerner Publications Company
A division of Lerner Publishing Group, Inc.
241 First Avenue North
Minneapolis, MN 55401 USA

For reading levels and more information, look up this title at www.lernerbooks.com.

Library of Congress Cataloging-in-Publication Data

Boothroyd, Jennifer, 1972–
    Why do moving objects slow down? : a look at friction / by Jennifer Boothroyd.
        p.   cm. — (Lightning bolt books™—Exploring physical science)
    Includes index.
    ISBN 978–0–7613–5432–1 (lib. bdg. : alk. paper)
    ISBN 978–0–7613–6298–2 (EB pdf)
    1. Friction—Juvenile literature. I. Title.
    QC197.B58 2011
    531'.4—dc22   2009048387

Manufactured in the United States of America
3 - 38541 - 10987 - 12/16/2016

Contents

What Is Friction?

Friction is a force created by rubbing.

A baseball player rubs against the ground while sliding into home plate.

Friction slows things down or makes them stop.

A player stops moving forward when he rubs against the ground.

A toy car creates friction when it rolls across the floor. Its wheels rub on the floor. The rubbing makes the car slow down and stop.

Friction is the reason a toy car eventually stops. Without friction, the car would keep on rolling and rolling.

Some surfaces have many bumps and grooves. These surfaces are rough. **They make a lot of friction.**

Carpet makes a lot of friction. If you rolled a toy car across this carpet, the car would quickly stop.

Other surfaces have few bumps and grooves. These surfaces are smooth. They make just a little friction.

Ice makes only a little friction. That's why stopping on ice skates can be tricky.

Every surface makes some amount of friction. That's because every surface has some bumps and grooves.

This glass goldfish bowl is very smooth. But even glass has bumps and grooves.

Friction in Water and Air

Water is a liquid. An object makes friction when it moves through a liquid.

These dolphins make friction as they swim through the water. Their skin rubs against the water.

Friction in the water slows objects down or makes them stop, just like it does on land.

Friction slows swimmers down.

The outside of a boat is smooth. A smooth boat makes little friction in the water. The boat can go fast.

Swimmers wear smooth swimsuits and caps. Swimmers can swim faster if they make little friction.

An object makes friction when it moves through a gas. Air is made of gases. Friction in the air is called air resistance. Air resistance slows things down or makes them stop.

This leaf floats slowly to the ground because of air resistance.

Air resistance slows down this parachute. Air resistance lets parachutes drift gently to the ground.

Air resistance slows down cars and trucks too. Air rubs against the vehicles as they move.

Friction and Weight

Heavier objects make more friction. It is easy to pull an empty sled. The sled rests lightly on the ground. There is little friction.

A sled with someone on it pushes hard against the ground.

There is a lot of friction. You need to use a strong force to pull the sled.

It takes a lot of force to pull this sled!

Good and Bad Friction

Friction can be very helpful.
Friction keeps us from slipping.

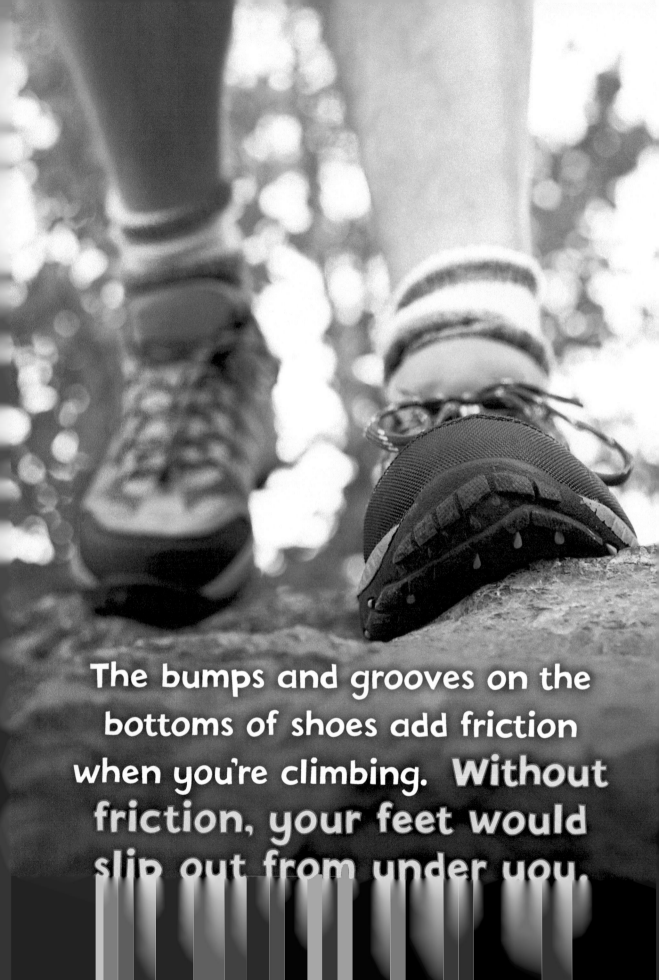

The bumps and grooves on the bottoms of shoes add friction when you're climbing. Without friction, your feet would slip out from under you.

Friction also helps us grip a bottle cap. The bumps and grooves in our skin make friction. So do the grooves on the bottle cap. The friction stops our fingers from slipping off the cap.

When you're unscrewing a bottle cap, you don't want your fingers to move. You want them to stay in place so that you can open the cap.

Friction can be a problem too. Friction makes heat. You may have seen this if you've ever rubbed your hands together. The rubbing creates heat. But too much heat can make machines start on fire.

Friction made this car engine overheat.

Cars use more gas because of friction. This driver steps on the gas when air resistance slows her car down. Stepping on the gas makes the car go faster. But cars pollute when they use a lot of gas.

Stepping on the gas makes a car give off pollution.

Lubrication

Lubrication can reduce friction. Lubrication is created by putting a slippery substance such as oil on an object. The slippery substance smoothes the object.

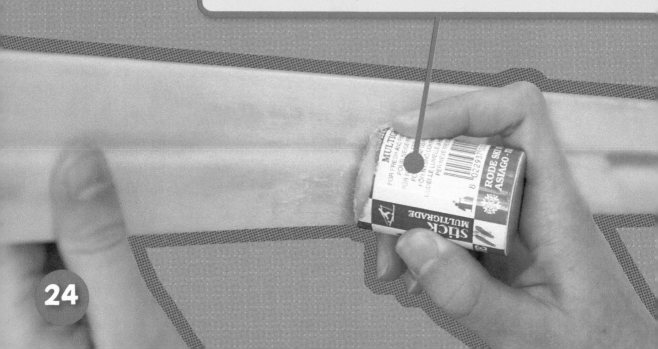

Putting wax on skis gives the skis less friction. Then the skis can move quickly on the snow.

Putting grease on a bike chain gives the chain less friction.

Putting water on a plastic slide gives the slide less friction.

Friction is an important force.

People need it
to work, travel,
and play.

Activity
Get a Grip

A gymnast powders his hands before grabbing the rings. A batter wears gloves when she holds the bat. The powder and the gloves both create more friction. Friction helps you grip objects.

How do different substances affect your ability to grip? Try this experiment to find out.

What you need:
a marble

a plastic sandwich bag

a metal spoon

ice cubes

a hand towel

talcum powder

vegetable oil

What you do:

1. Use your thumb and pointer finger to pick up the marble. Then pick up the sandwich bag, the metal spoon, and an ice cube. Which objects were the easiest to pick up? Which were the hardest?

2. Dry your hand with the towel if it's wet from picking up the ice. Now dip your finger and thumb in the talcum powder. Pick up the objects again. Were any easier or harder to pick up?

3. Clean and dry your hand. Next, dip your finger and thumb in the vegetable oil. Once again, try picking up all the objects. Were any easier or harder to pick up this time?

Glossary

air resistance: friction caused when an object moves in the air

force: a push or a pull

friction: a force that slows things down or makes them stop. Rubbing creates friction.

gas: a substance that will spread to fill any space that contains it

liquid: a wet substance that you can pour

lubrication: putting a slippery substance such as oil on an object

pollute: to make the land, the air, or the water dirty

surface: the outside of something

Further Reading

BBC Bitesize Science: Friction
http://www.bbc.co.uk/schools/ks2bitesize/science/
physical_processes/friction/play.shtml

Dragonfly TV: Ice Bike
http://pbskids.org/dragonflytv/show/icebike.html

Driscoll, Laura. *Slow Down, Sara!* New York: Kane
Press, 2003.

Riley, Peter D. *Forces and Friction.* North Mankato,
MN: Smart Apple Media, 2008.

Trumbauer, Lisa. *What Is Friction?* New York:
Children's Press, 2004.

Whitehouse, Patty. *Good Friction, Bad Friction.*
Vero Beach, FL: Rourke, 2007.

Index

Photo Acknowledgments

The images in this book are used with the permission of: © iStockphoto.com/Yenwen Lu, p. 2; © Tetra Images/Getty Images, p. 4; © Mike Powell/All Sports Concepts/Getty Images, p. 5; Reflexstock/First Light/Huy Lam, p. 6; © Indeed/Aflo/Getty Images, p. 7; © William Stevenson/SuperStock, p. 8; © Imagesource/Photolibrary, p. 9; © Paul Souders/Getty Images, p. 10; © Thomas Barwick/Taxi/Getty Images, p. 11; © iStockphoto.com/Dan Barnes, p. 12; © Radius images/Getty Images, p. 13; © Corey Hilz/DanitaDelimont.com, p. 14; © Vibrant Image Studio/Shutterstock Images, p. 15; © Maciej Nowkowski/istock exclusive/Getty Images, p. 16; © Andrew Geiger/Taxi/Getty Images, p. 17; © Mike Timo/Stone/Getty Images, p. 18; © iStockphoto.com/ND1939, p. 19; Tommy Hanratty/Fancy/Photolibrary, p. 20; © Marc Volk/fStop/Alamy, p. 21; © iStockphoto.com/Joe Belanger , p. 22; © Julie Caruso, pp. 23, 24; © Stephan Hoeck/Getty Images, p. 25; © Amy Steigbigel/Getty Images, p. 26; © R. Gino Santa Maria/Shutterstock Images, p. 27; © Dyscoh/ Dreamstime.com, p. 28 (plastic bag); © Newlight/Dreamstime.com, p. 28 (vegetable oil); © Design56/Dreamstime.com, p. 28 (talcum powder); © sushi/Shutterstock Images, p. 28 (hand towel); © Leonr/Dreamstime.com, p. 28 (ice cubes); © O.V.D./Shutterstock Images, p. 28 (spoon); © Aquariagir/Dreamstime.com, p. 28 (marble); © Glow Images, p. 30; © Celia Peterson/Photolibrary, p. 31.

Front cover: AP Photo/Doug Mills.